Passing the Point

by

Bernard McCall

INTRODUCTION

Battery Point at Portishead has long been a popular vantage area for watching ships sailing past on their way to or from the port areas of Bristol and Sharpness. The Point has a fine position and because of this was deemed to be a vital part of Bristol's defences. A watchtower stood at the Point in Elizabethan times. In the mid-17th century, Portishead Fort, as it was known then, was defended by a local garrison of Cavaliers during the Civil War. More fortifications were added in Napoleonic times, and during the two world wars of the last century anti-submarine defences were placed here. Battery Point lighthouse will be seen in several photographs in this book. It was built in 1931 and its bell was added a few years later.

The phenomenal growth of the Port of Bristol during the 1990s has resulted in a wider variety of ships to be seen than ever before, many of these ships being of a size almost unimaginable in the 1950s. It is the purpose of this book to present a sample selection of these vessels and to write enough about them to be of interest to general readers and enthusiasts alike. For the information of general readers, the letters and numbers after the name of each ship indicate its flag, its gross tonnage and its year of build. This information will be familiar to enthusiasts.

Most of the photographs are mine, but those marked DMc have been taken by my son, Dominic. I am grateful to him for supplementing my own views in this way. I also wish to thank the staff and crews of Svitzer Marine Ltd for their help. Thanks must also go to Alasdair Moodie, of Osprey Shipping; Mike Tree, of Clarkson Brothers; and Peter Hobday, formerly of Denholm Shipping, for their help in providing information, and to Gil Mayes who has checked for errors. The book could not have been written without assistance from Bristol Port Company, notably Paul White in the Commercial Department, and Patrick Kearon who has been kind enough to write the Foreword.

Bernard McCall, Portishead

January 2005

FOREWORD

In the hurly-burly of day-to-day life in a busy port, it is difficult, even for those involved in its operation, to find the time to see and also to remember the ships that come and go each year. Bernard McCall, through his well-researched books, helps jog the memory for us in this respect. He provides the same service for those many enthusiasts who, also because of the pressures of time, are unable to watch and enjoy all the ships that, each tide, pass close to the Portishead's Battery Point.

The author, with camera and pen, lays out fascinating and detailed snapshots of those vessels of all sizes and types. All at Bristol Port are delighted that he has done so, and look forward to more of the same in the future.

Niels Westberg, Haven Master, Bristol Port.

*Front cover : Amongst the most eye-catching of the ships to have passed Battery Point in recent years are the white container ships operated by the South African shipping company Safmarine. As will be seen elsewhere in the book, more modern container ships chartered by Safmarine now arrive on a regular basis and the very few calls by the "White Ladies" were eagerly awaited. It was on a gloriously sunny 14 December 2003 that the **S A Sederberg** (BHS, 52615gt/78) made her way towards Royal Portbury Dock at the end of a voyage from Cape Town.*

*Back cover : The Ukrainian cruise liner **Azerbaydzhan** sails into the summer sunset on 5 September 1994. Further information about this ship will be found on page 4.*

passage of cruise vessels past Battery Point is guaranteed to ensure a large ber of onlookers both on the Point and along Portishead's waterfront. It is the ing departure of the ships which is most popular. Although there are many st attractions within a 25-mile radius of the port, the number of cruise ships g has been surprisingly small. On the morning of 14 July 1998, the **Royal** **Viking Sun** (BHS, 37845gt/88) heads towards Bristol from Falmouth, departing for Dublin later in the day . This cruise ship was built for Royal Viking Line by Wärtsilä Marine Industries at Turku, Finland, and entered the Cunard fleet when the latter took over Royal Viking Line. From 1999, she traded as **Seabourn Sun** but currently sails under the name **Prinsendam**.

The departure of the ***Azerbaydzhan*** (UKR, 15410gt/75) on 5 September 1994 was watched by a very large crowd at Battery Point. Arriving from Liverpool earlier that day, she was the first cruise vessel to visit the port for many years. Sadly, though, the cruise was marred by controversy because she suffered a cockroach infestation. In herself, she is an interesting ship. She is one of five sisterships built by Oy Wärtsilä at Turku in Finland as a multi-purpose ships with doors and ramps at bow and stern and on the starboard side, thus allowing as a ferry if required. In this configuration, the ships had accommodation for passengers in berths and 504 unberthed. She had further accommodation a in 1986 and was subsequently able to offer 650 berths. She currently tr under the name ***Enchanted Capri***.

he time that the **Silver Wind** (BHS, 16927gt/95) was passing the Point on the ning of 27 June 1995, the sunlight was illuminating her starboard side rather the port side which shore-based onlookers could see. At this time, she was a fairly new vessel having been completed earlier in the year by Italian shipbuilders. Three different shipyards had been involved in her construction, final work being carried out at the Esercizio yard in Viareggio.

Perhaps the most familiar vessels to be seen passing Battery Point are vehicle carriers. Not the most attractive of ships, they nevertheless are a vital source of income for the port and indeed for the whole local area. The ships operated by the Japanese company Nippon Yusen Kaisha (NYK) are recognisable by their funnel colours of black with two narrow red bands on a broad white band. The company operates bulk carriers and tankers in addition to vehicle carriers. *Fuji* (LBR, 47751gt/84), was built by Imabari Zosen K K at Marugame. Sh▨ seen heading towards Royal Portbury Dock on 28 April 1996 bringing 1088 c▨ The scene is completed by anglers on the shoreline and small yachts ta▨ advantage of the spring breeze.

ne is the abbreviated title of Kawasaki Kisen Kaisha Ltd, Tokyo, a member of Far Eastern Freight Conference. Its ships are characterised by the large white r K on a red funnel. The **Franconia** (LIB, 36201gt/85) bears the name of a famous Cunard vessel of yesteryear. She was built by Imabari Zosen K K, at Marugame. She was photographed on 8 June 1996 as she headed for Royal Portbury Dock with 991 cars including Honda and Daewoo models.

The vehicle carriers of Grimaldi Lines have become a frequent sight over the years. One of the older examples of the company's fleet is the **Arno** (ITA, 25312gt/73) built at the P Smit Jr yard in Rotterdam. As will be seen, this in itself is unusual as the vast majority of these vessels have been built in the Far East, usually Japan or South Korea. The **Arno** is able to carry about 3500 cars. Sh inward bound on a June day in 1994. At the end of 2003, she was rename **Angelo** and still trades into Royal Portbury Dock. Interestingly, another Grim vessel named after a river, the **Po**, traded as **St Angelo** between 2000 and 20

The pale orange hulls of the current Grimaldi fleet are very distinctive and examples visit Royal Portbury Dock two or three times each week. There is often departure on a Friday. The **Grand Benelux** (ITA, 37800gt/01) was built at the Uljanik shipyard in Pula. She has 11 decks, 3 of which are hoistable and, with a lane length of 3100 metres, can carry 4310 cars. She approaches Royal Portbury Dock from Valencia on 30 November 2003 with a cargo of 2500 cars, mainly Ford models built in Spain. She departed for Sheerness the next day. Some of these

Grimaldi vessels accept passengers for either a one-week voyage from Bristol to other ports in northern Europe or longer voyages varying between 28 and 35 days visiting ports in the Mediterranean as well as a selection of northern European ports. Most of the newer ships in the Grimaldi fleet are named with the prefix "Grand" or "Grande" followed by a country or port served by the line's many services.

Wallenius Lines is a Swedish company the majority of whose ships are named after operas such as *Traviata* or *Aida*. However a small number have more prosaic names with the suffix "Breeze" and the ***Atlantic Breeze*** (SGP, 41891/86) is one of these. Owned by a Wallenius subsidiary company in Singapore, the ship was built by Kanasashi Co Ltd, at Toyohashi. She has a car capacity of 489 vehicles and two of her ten decks are fitted with hoists. These decks can thus b raised to allow taller vehicles to be conveyed. The photograph was taken on 2 July 2000 when she delivered a cargo of Mitsubishi cars.

...presenting the Wilhelmsen fleet is the **Tai Shan** (NIS, 48676gt/86), built by ...nitomo Heavy Industries at Yokosuka. She can carry over 5800 cars on her ...lve decks, four of which can be raised. Wilhelmsen is a long-established ...wegian shipping company whose ships have always been identifiable by the ...narrow blue bands on a black funnel. The fleet nowadays consists almost exclusively of vehicle carriers. The photograph was taken in Spring 2000 when she arrived with 813 cars including Honda and Suzuki models. Her first visit to the Bristol Channel was in March 1996 when she was named **Nosac Tai Shan**, the word Nosac standing for Norwegian Specialist Auto Carriers. At the time of writing, she has made eighteen voyages to Royal Portbury Dock.

The grey-hulled vehicle carriers of United European Car Carriers (UECC) visit the port at the rate of two or three each week. Illustrating an earlier generation of small vehicle carrier is the **Autocarrier** (ATF, 6421gt/82), built at the Flender Werft yard in Lübeck. At the time of the photograph, July 1993, she was registered at Grimstad in Norway but this was subsequently changed to Port-aux- Francais in the French Antarctic Territories. The activities of boats belonging Portishead Sailing Club are well monitored by fast rescue launches but pleasure craft visiting Portishead Marina or sailing further up channel Sharpness can sometimes cause anxious moments for the pilots of commer vessels.

Autostar (NIS, 21010gt/00) is an example of the latest generation of vehicle carriers in the UECC fleet. Built by the Tsuneishi Shipbuilding Co Ltd at makuma in Japan, she can accommodate 1900 cars and has an impressive vice speed of almost 21 knots. When outward bound on an ebbing tide, these ssels make a very fine sight as they speed down channel. This photograph was taken on 17 January 2004. During 2004 this vessel has been a frequent visitor from the port of Pasajes in northern Spain, carrying mainly Vauxhall Corsa cars. On the return voyage, she carries Rover cars, Land Rovers and Range Rovers along with Jaguar and UK-produced General Motors cars for the Iberian market. (DMc)

An operator whose vessels are seen only occasionally in the Bristol Channel is Lineas Suardiaz. On 30 March 2003, the **Olivia** (BHS, 6461gt/82) heads for Dublin having discharged cars from Zeebrugge. At the time, she was trading regularly from the latter port to Bristol and Dublin. She can carry 750 cars and w' built at the Duro Felguera yard in Gijon. Throughout 2003, Suardiaz ran a wee service bringing French-built Toyota Yaris models for the UK market. (DMc)

charter to Lineas Suardiaz at the time of this photograph, taken in July 1994, the *Feedercrew* (MLT, 3641gt/72). She has an interesting history for she built by Schulte & Bruns at Emden as a roll-on/roll-off ship for use in the er trade from Scandinavia. As such, she was named *Hallstavik*. In 1991, she was sold, renamed *Feedercrew*, and converted to a vehicle carrier with a capacity for 340 cars. The line's ships were regular visitors in the mid-1990s ferrying Polish-built Fiat Cinquecento models from German ports into Royal Portbury Dock.

It is difficult to know how to categorise the **Tapiola** (NIS, 39535gt/78). She is certainly a multi-purpose ship and is classified by *Lloyd's Register* as a roll on / roll off container ship. She can accommodate 580 cars and has a container capacity of 2000 TEU, including 120 refrigerated containers. She was built by Mitsubishi Heavy Industries Limited at Nagasaki and was operated on the Wallenius Wilhelmsen "around-the-world" service. On the homeward leg from the US Gulf and east coast, she loaded forest products for discharge at Royal Portbury Dock. On this voyage, she carried nearly 10,000 tonnes of woodp Kraft Liner board (used in packaging), and plywood. She now trades around Pacific basin. A similar Wilhelmsen vessel, the **Tampa**, hit the world's headl after her Master picked up refugees and was refused permission to doc Australia. The tug **Portgarth** prepares to assist her as she heads up cha bound for Royal Portbury Dock on 6 September 1997.

en she left Royal Portbury Dock bound for Amsterdam on 15 August 1994, the *otain Veniamis* (MLT, 68178gt/72) was the biggest ship to have visited the k and her departure was well-publicised, resulting in a large crowd gathering a warm summer day to watch her pass. She had arrived from Ponta da Madeira in Brazil four days previously with a part cargo of 46,556 tonnes of soya for animal feed. Built by Mitsubishi Heavy Industries at Hiroshima, she was eventually sold to Indian shipbreakers and arrived at Alang on 24 July 1998.

With a length of 266 metres, the *Fernie* (BMU, 63153gt/96) is one of the biggest ships to call at Royal Portbury Dock and she is seen passing Battery Point on with a cargo of 105,655 tonnes of coal from Baltimore. She was built by Daewoo Heavy Industries at Okpo, and has nine holds and nine hatches. At the time of this visit on 27 April 1997, she was owned by P&O but she was later to be s by this company. She has made a total of eight visits to our local port, six of th with cargoes of coal from Australia. She utilises six tugs on her approach to port, four of these helping to put her on to her berth once in Royal Portbury D

arly 1994, there was a new source of coal when the **Sir Charles Parsons** R, 14201gt/85) brought some cargoes from the River Tyne. She made een visits to the port in 1994 carrying coal to the Bristol Bulk Terminal. This ity is a joint venture with power generator RWE npower, the successor to the nal partner, National Power. The ship was built by Govan Shipbuilders Ltd for UK's nationalised electricity company, called at the time the Central Electricity erating Board. Following privatisation, part of this company became

Powergen the vessel was wearing Powergen colours as she passed Battery Point in February 1994. She is one of three similar ships which are usually to be found delivering coal to Kingsnorth Power Station on the River Medway, formerly a Powergen generating station but now owned by E. On. The ship is named after a Tyneside engineer who designed the first steam-powered turbine ship, called appropriately **Turbinia**.

Another bulk carrier importing coal on a fairly regular basis over the past two years has been the **Santa Vitoria** (PAN, 40030gt/02), built in Japan by the Tsuneishi Shipbuilding Co Ltd at Numakuma. She is seen on 14 January 2004 as she arrives from Murmansk, not a usual source of coal imports most of which come from Richards Bay in South Africa and occasionally from Australia. The s sailed for New Orleans four days later. When they are approaching the port, I carriers will have one tug at the bow, two at the stern, and, depending on the s either one or two tugs pushing at the ship's starboard side.

operly classed as a mini-bulker, the **Saint Brevin** (PAN, 3885gt/75) passes up annel on her to discharge a cargo of cement for Castle Cement Ltd in onmouth in October 1993. A product of the Kleven shipyard in Ulsteinvik, she ded as **Refsnes** until 1983 and then was renamed **Saint Brevin**. She reverted nost to her original name when she was renamed **Refnes** in 2000. There have been very few cement cargoes since the mid-1990s when Castle concentrated on UK production rather than importing from its Scandinavian owner Scancem. The company is now owned by Heidelberg, a major German cement manufacturer.

The other commodity which is brought to Royal Portbury Dock in large bulk carriers is animal feed. The **Etoile** (PAN, 64785gt/77) is one of the longest vessels to visit the port with a length of over 267 metres and has made several calls in recent years. She generally loads at Destrehan on the Mississippi, not far from New Orleans. She is chartered by Arkady Feeds and carries American corn gluten for animal feed compounders in the West Country. On this visit she carried 48,735 tonnes of animal feed. She was built at the Götaverken shipyard in Landskrona, Sweden. She was photographed as she made the custom cautious approach on 22 June 2004. That such large vessels can be brought the port with little apparent difficulty is a credit to the pilots and tug crews w handle the ships with consummate skill. A tug always escorts these large vess from the English and Welsh Grounds buoy and other tugs will make fast to ship as she enters Walton Bay at the Welsh Hook buoy.

(DM

iving from Antwerp on 10 August 2004 to load a cargo of 31,500 tonnes of ap metal for the US Gulf is the **Georgete K** (GRC, 20276gt/84) built by subishi Heavy Industries at Kobe. She is a typical Japanese-built bulk carrier he mid-1980s, many of these being built for the carriage of timber. The rails d stanchions on her deck protect such cargoes. She has five holds and five ches which are served by four cranes each able to lift 25 tons. Simsmetal have operated a metal processing and export terminal at Avonmouth since Spring 1988. The stockyard is on the site of a former granary demolished to make way for the development. Scrap vehicles and steel are shredded before being exported to a number of countries including Spain, Turkey, India and Pakistan for reprocessing.

The Lafarge plasterboard factory, one of the largest developments on the industrial estate at Portbury, generates a demand for the import of gypsum. It is linked to the quayside at Berth 4 by an overhead conveyor system into which the ship discharges its cargo. In the mid-1990s, the **Wani Swan** (PAN, 14387gt/77) was a regular caller with cargoes of 22,000 tonnes of gypsum loaded at Carboneras on the Mediterranean coast of Spain. Built as a conventional bulk carrier by Imabari Zosen K K at Marugame, she was converted to a self-discharging bulk carrier in 1990 by Wani Shipping A/S, of Oslo. Her discharging gear is on the port side of the ship but much of it is visible in this view as she passes Battery Point on 5 August 1995.

ce 2001 imports of gypsum have been brought from Garrucha, not far from
boneras, by the much-larger **Yeoman Bank** (LBR, 24870gt82), built by
usis Shipyards in Greece. She too has been converted to a self-discharging
sel from a conventional bulk carrier, her conversion coming in 1991. Her
ne suggests a connection with Foster Yeoman - she is owned by this company
through Aggregate Carriers Ltd. When not carrying gypsum, she generally loads
stone at Foster Yeoman's huge Glensanda quarry in Scotland for distribution
throughout Europe. She passes the Point on 24 April 2004 carrying 35,875
tonnes of rock gypsum. She normally discharges within 48 hours of berthing.

The **Canterbury Star** (BHS, 10291gt/86) had brought her cargo of fresh produce all the way from New Zealand and had left Napier on 22 April 2004, passing the Panama Canal and arriving at Avonmouth on 18 May. She was in port only briefly for she is seen here leaving port later that same day. On this visit she carried a part cargo of 400 pallets of apples. Built for Blue Star Line and having a pr[...] which will be familiar to many ship enthusiasts, she is a product of the Harlan[...] Wolff shipyard in Belfast and she has retained her original name although [...] working for other owners.

The **Orange Star** (LBR, 9981gt/75) is another former member of the Blue Star fleet for she was built at Smith's Dock on the River Tees as **Andalucia Star**. In 1987, she was converted from a conventional refrigerated cargo ship to a tanker/cargo ship designed to carry fruit juice in six cargo tanks at a minimum temperature of -12 degrees Celsius. She is still able to carry conventional cargo in one hold and in the tweendeck spaces. She is becoming a regular visitor to Avonmouth delivering concentrated orange juice from Brazil to the recently-completed European Juice Terminal. After storage the juice is delivered by road tanker to packing plants where it is put into cartons before delivery to the retailers.

The local media announced that a new trade was brought to the port on 27 March 2003 when the **Pacific Reefer** (PAN, 10991gt/99) arrived with palletised fresh fruit from Valparaiso in Chile. In fact, the port has handled many refrigerated cargoes over the years, including bananas from the West Indies by Geest Line in the early 1980s. It was also not strictly true to say that the arrival of this vessel inaugurated the new trade for a trial shipment had been brought two weeks earlier by the **Anglian Reefer**. The port has converted one of its modern sheds, formerly known as S Shed, into a fresh produce terminal. The store's nine temperature-controlled compartments are capable of holding 8,000 pallets of fr and vegetables. The terminal is being doubled in size for the 2005 season. T **Pacific Reefer** was built by Shin Kochi Jyuko K K, at Kochi in Japan. She operated by LauritzenCool, a Swedish-based associate company of the huge Lauritzen shipping group which includes tankers and bulk carriers. Because the seasonal nature of many refrigerated trades, the company's ships a designed to carry return cargoes such as cars to the loading areas.

(DM

e now look at some of the general cargo ships which have been viewed over e last decade. On 5 January 1997, the **Snowbird** (VCT, 17728gt/73) heads up annel bound for Avonmouth from China with 6000 tonnes of rapeseed pellets for the animal feed industry. She departed for Glasgow three days later. The ship was renamed *Yi Ling* later in 1997 and was sold for demolition in India in 1998, arriving at the scrapyard on 19 December 1998.

Regular callers with forest products are ships operated within the Gearbulk consortium, a shipping company founded in 1968 by four well-established companies. Forest products are one of the mainstays of Portbury's trade. Indeed the first commercial ship to visit the then new port on 12 April 1978 was Gearbulk's *Kiwi Arrow*, carrying plywood and woodpulp from British Columbia. The *Harefield* (27818gt/85) was built by Hyundai Heavy Industries at Ulsan.

These ships are on a round-the-world service and the *Harefield* would dischar[ge] elsewhere in northern Europe, possibly Antwerp and/or Szczecin. Parcels [of] packaged timber are in evidence as deck cargo as the ship makes her way do[wn the] channel on 30 April 2000 having discharged a part cargo of mainly woodp[ulp] loaded in British Columbia. Gearbulk continues to operate this service along w[ith] a monthly arrival from South Africa.

e the bulk carrier **Santa Vitoria** seen on page 20, the **Barbet Arrow** (BHS, 70gt/85) was built by the Tsuneishi Shipbuilding Co Ltd at Numakuma. ough a typical Gearbulk ship with Gearbulk name, she does not carry that pany's name on her hull. She was photographed on 27 March 1999. The s are examples of a type known as open-hatch gantry-craned, and Gearbulk rates about 35% of the world's capacity of this type of ship. Both the

Harefield and **Barbet Arrow** are examples of the fourth generation of these vessels in the Gearbulk fleet. The **Barbet Arrow** was formerly the **City of New Westminster** and was operated by the Canadian Transport Company (CTCo) carrying forest products from British Columbia to north European ports. CTCo was acquired by Gearbulk in late 1998 and the ship was then renamed.

With the navigation light and bell in evidence, the **Atlanta Forest** (MLT, 12582gt/78) passes the Point in January 1994. The ship was built at the Juliana Constructora shipyard in Gijon and was one of three virtually identical ships built for Finnish owners. She visited Avonmouth twice in 1994 carrying aluminium the UK market. On this visit she brought 5,255 tonnes. The ship continue trade under the name **Kent Forest**.

Anangel Fidelity (GRC, 14156gt/79) is yet another ship built in Japan, in case at Aioi by Ishikawajima-Harima Heavy Industry Co Ltd. A particular ure of this ship are the two gantry cranes of unusual design and able to lift 22 tonnes. The ship has five holds which are served by eight hatches. She is seen inward bound from Cartagena in Colombia on 22 February 1998 carrying a part cargo of 2800 tonnes of tissue paper destined for use in UK bathrooms.

Heading up channel on 18 June 1995 is the **Philia** (MLT, 3228gt/72). She will discharge 7700 tonnes of animal feed into the store of Agricultural Bulk Services (ABS) at Portbury. ABS was originally a joint venture between Tate & Lyle and the Bristol Port Company but is now wholly owned by the Port Company. The fac has four large sheds capable of storing 200,000 tonnes of feed. The ship v sold for demolition in late 2001, arriving at Sachana in India on 2 December.

Marika Stravelakis (LBR, 13538gt/72) heads down channel on the late ernoon of 23 November 1996. She was almost at the end of her career under name for she was sold and renamed *Grigoroussa* on 30 December. She had delivered 12,000 tonnes of Chilean concentrates loaded in Antofagasta for Britannia Zinc's smelting works in Avonmouth. After many years of production, this plant was closed in the summer of 2003 and has since been demolished.

One fact that will be apparent in the pages of this book is the number of ships built in the Far East. The **Le Ding** (CHN, 15525gt/98) was built at Dalian Shipyard and is indeed owned in China. Her four holds are served by eight hatches and careful observation of her deck cranes reveals that the middle crane of the three is rather more substantial than the other two. This can lift 40 tonnes compared to the 15 tonnes of the smaller cranes. She was outbound from Royal Portb Dock to Rotterdam on 9 February 2003, having arrived two days previously fr Xingang. She had brought 3600 tonnes of scaffold tubes manufactured in Ch for use here in the building industry.

(DN

In the 1970s and 1980s, vessels such as the **Kaliningrad** (RUS, 2736gt/69) were common sight in ports throughout Europe, generally carrying cargoes of timber which they were designed. She is one of a large class built between the late 60s and early 1970s at a time when Soviet shipyards could not cope with the number of orders placed by the state nationalised shipping company. Many orders were placed outside Russia, especially neighbouring Finland. The

Kaliningrad was built at the Valmet shipyard in Turku. By the late 1990s, such ships had often outlived their useful life and were sold on to other owners. It was in 1997 that the **Kaliningrad** was sold and renamed **Vita**. In late 2004, unlike many others of her type, she continues to trade. She is seen here outward bound on 2 September 1994 with an export cargo of barley from the West Country.

The **Kapitan Georgiy Baglay** (RUS, 11262gt/74) is a much larger vessel than the **Kaliningrad** but again represents a standard Russian design. She and twelve sisterships were built at the Chernomenskiy shipyard in Nikolaev between 1969 and 1975. She heads towards Avonmouth in April 1994 with 12,500 ton of animal feed. Sold and renamed **Julia IV** in 1997, she was scrapped at Ala India, in autumn 2000.

e **Nikos M** (CYP, 3895gt/75) is typical of very many ships built in Japan in the 70s. A product of the Asakawa Zosen K K yard at Imabari, she has two holds d two hatches which are served by four derricks each able to lift 15 tonnes. She seems to be in need of cosmetic attention as she heads towards Avonmouth on 4 June 1995 at the end of a voyage from Constanta with a part cargo of concentrates for the smelter of Britannia Zinc.

A new trade which began in 2003 is the import of jet fuel which is stored in tanks at Hallen, formerly used by the Ministry of Defence, and subsequently pumped to Heathrow Airport or delivered by road tanker to Bristol International, Cardiff and Exeter airports. More tanks situated on the outskirts of Portishead will be used from early 2005. The fuel is usually imported from refineries in the Middle East rather than in Europe and the **Sitacamilla** (NIS, 43406gt/88) arrived from the Saudi Arabian port of Jubail on 26 February 2004 with 67,851 tonnes of jet fu[el]. She was photographed from a less-frequently used vantage point as s[he] departed for Milford Haven two days later. She was built at the Copenhagen ya[rd] of B&W Skibsværft. The Bristol Aviation Fuel Terminal at Portbury was built in t[he] port's former pumping pond and was opened in May 2003.

ost of the photographs in this book were taken from Battery Point looking out to a, but here we are clearly on the water with Battery Point just visible at the far ht of the photograph. The tanker **British Energy** (GBR, 23682gt/01) is eparing to make her approach to Royal Portbury Dock on 10 June 2004 with a rt cargo of 15,000 tonnes of jet fuel from Texas City. She sailed the next day to scharge the balance of her cargo at BP's storage tanks at the Isle of Grain on the River Medway. The stern tug **Svitzer Brunel** is just securing a line to her. This crucial manoeuvre requires excellent understanding between the tug crew, the pilot on the ship and the ship's crew. The tanker is one of a pair of sisterships built at the Daedong shipyard in Chinhae.

(DMc)

The funnel marking of this tanker is self-explanatory for she is named **Orange Star** (NIS, 18302gt/76). She was built at the Verolme shipyard, Alblasserdam, near Rotterdam. She was photographed in Spring 1997 when she arrived with a 9,000 tonne cargo of molasses to discharge at the SVG Intermol terminal on t foreshore at Avonmouth. Molasses has been imported into Bristol for many yea and is used primarily as a sweetener and binder by animal feed manufacturer

he *Orange Star* on page 27 was a converted vessel, the *Orange Blossom* 3R, 9984gt/85) is a tanker purpose-built for the carriage of fruit juice. She was nstructed at the Trosvik Verksted yard in Brevik. On 11 September 2004, a very owery day, a gap in the cloud and a shaft of sunlight were sufficient to give a npse of a rainbow at a suitable moment as the ship headed towards Avonmouth at the end of a voyage from Santos. She had already discharged a part-cargo of fruit juice in Rotterdam. After a three-day stay in port, she sailed for Brazil to load another cargo which was to arrive in Avonmouth just over one month later.

The arrival of the Russian tanker *Alekseevka* (3142gt/65) in autumn 1994 brought a long-outdated profile to the port for tankers with bridge/accommodation amidships were very rarely seen in UK ports at that time. She was an example of a large class of tankers built for Russia at the Rauma-Repola shipyard in the Finnish port of Rauma between 1961 and 1967. She was carrying a cargo 25 tonnes of molasses, a commodity which is often brought by interesting ol tankers from ports such as Ravenna or Karachi. Pakistan is now the larg molasses exporter in the world.

ring the 1990s, gas tankers arrived regularly to load liquefied petroleum gas, by-product of land-based oil wells operated by BP at Wytch Farm in Dorset. e gas was delivered mainly to Drogheda on the east coast of Ireland and xoes in Portugal. A frequent caller was the **Kilgas Pioneer** (CYP, 1173gt/92), lt at the Alblas shipyard in Hendrik-Ido-Ambacht, south of Rotterdam. Her lpg cargo is carried in four horizontal tanks made of stainless steel. This view is dated 30 May 1997 and she was carrying 740 tonnes of lpg. Later in the year, the ship was sold and renamed **Gas Pioneer**. She made 48 voyages from Avonmouth as the **Kilgas Pioneer** but just one more under her new name.

By mid-1995, construction of the new Severn Bridge was well underway and some of the work can be seen in the background of this photograph of the gas tanker **Snowdon** (SGP, 3219gt/89) heading down channel on 27 August 1995. She was heading for the Leixoes in Portugal with 1650 tonnes of lpg. She was built at Imabari in Japan by Higaki Zosen K K. The steel work for the new bridge was manufactured in Italy and shipped from Porto Nogaro, near Venice, Avonmouth before being delivered to the construction site at Pilning.

Burntisland Shipbuilding Co Ltd had its yard on the northern shore of the
n of Forth and built many vessels for British owners. The **Frank M** (GBR,
1gt/65) was constructed for Metcalf Motor Coasters whose vessels were
racterised by the white letter M on green funnel. She had been in service for
ost thirty years when she was photographed inward bound at Battery Point on
994. She made four visits to Avonmouth during that year, all with 1600 tonnes
of mixed petroleum products for Bristol Oil Storage Ltd. She was sold the
following year and was renamed **God Premium**. The ever-growing need for
petroleum products over the last decade has meant that tankers in the coastal
distribution trades from refineries such as those at Milford Haven and Fawley to
other ports have become much larger.

This tanker just had to be included because of her name! The **Avon 1** (VCT, 2643gt/71) was photographed inward bound from the River Tees in April 1997 shortly after being renamed from **Orion**. This was, in fact, her first voyage under her new name. She was built at the Voldnes shipyard in Forsnavåg, Norway, and is classed as a chemical tanker. She is fitted with heating coils in her twe tanks, allowing her to carry heavy fuel oils. Indeed this was her cargo for she w carrying 3000 tonnes of feedstock for the local carbon black factory of Sevale

minent amongst the tankers which bring refined products from Milford Haven the vessels operated by the James Fisher company in Barrow-in-Furness, this member of the fleet is not one of the company's usual tankers to be found he Bristol Channel. The **Thames Fisher** (GBR, 2760gt/97) is not only owned registered in Barrow but was built at the Vickers shipyard in that town. In this view she is heading back to Milford Haven on 2 October 1999. Of special note is the extent of activity at the Llanwern steel works in the background. Little was it realised at that time that this huge works would close within four years - another nail in the coffin of British manufacturing industry.

The **Safmarine Nahoon** (DEU, 16264gt/97) was built in Poland by Stocznia Szczecinska. She has a container capacity of 1684 TEU of which 630 may be in her holds and 1054 on deck. Her three cranes can each lift 45 tonnes. Like many purpose-built container vessels of her type, she has had a series of names reflecting the identity of her charterers. She was built as **Nordcoast** but took names associated with charterers on three occasions between 1997 and 2002, each time reverting to her original name on completion of the charter except in late February 2002 when she changed directly from **DAL East London** to

Safmarine Nahoon. Here we see her heading for Royal Portbury Dock at end of a voyage from South Africa via Lisbon on 22 October 2002. She car 130 full boxes containing mainly Mercedes Benz cars manufactured in So Africa. She loaded 207 empty boxes before leaving for Bremerhaven via Antw three days later and she reverted to the name **Nordcoast** at the German por 8 November. The stern view of the ship affords a view of the funnel carry traditional Safmarine colours.

otographed from the roadside at the Lake Grounds where there is ample free king for visitors, the **DAL Karoo** (DEU, 23896gt/98) was also built in Poland by Stocznia Gdynia. She wears the funnel colours of Deutsche Africa Line is a regular caller with containers from South Africa usually calling at East London, Durban, Cape Town and Port Elizabeth. There are also calls at Lisbon on both northbound and southbound voyages. The photograph was taken on 25 April 2004.

The Mediterranean Shipping Company Ltd, generally known by its shorter titles of Medite or MSC, is one of the world's largest carriers of containers by sea. Its vessels are usually to be seen in Europe's biggest ports and at Felixstowe. In Spring 2004, it announced a reorganisation of some of its services to Iberia and as a result four of the company's smaller container ships call regularly at Royal Portbury Dock en route to ports such as Vigo, Leixoes and Valencia, with calls at Antwerp on the outward route and Dublin and Belfast on the return. The **MSC** **Provence** (MLT, 17304gt/79) is one of the regular callers. She was buil Warnemünde and, like many container vessels, she has had several previ names and was trading as **City of Liverpool** until she took this name in 2003. She was on her way to Antwerp when photographed on 10 August 20 She made one further visit under this name before changing name to **M** **Erminia** for her call in October 2004.

hough the Bell Lines services had ceased, there was still a call for goods to be nsported on the routes the company had developed. One of the most :cessful routes was that linking Avonmouth to the Iberian peninsula and it was : long before Seawheel, a European logistics company, introduced a vessel o the route. The **Arklow Castle** (IRL, 5006gt/96) will be very familiar to the jular spectators at Battery Point for she often arrives on a Sunday. On her outward voyage to Bilbao, she includes calls at Greenock and Dublin but returns direct to Avonmouth. In recent years, this has been a joint service with Spanish company Vapores Suardiaz and more recently still she has carried containers for MacAndrews on a slot charter basis. Operated by Arklow Shipping, the vessel is one of several similar container ships built at the Hugo Peters shipyard in Wewelsfleth, just off the River Elbe.

When Bell Lines, an Irish transport and logistics company, transferred its short sea container services from its private Bellport on the River Usk to Avonmouth in 1993, there was great optimism that this would prove to be an important stage in the company's expansion. This optimism was initially fulfilled but various factors combined to bring about the demise of Bell Lines in 1997. There was no hint of the troubles that lay ahead when the **Bell Ruler** (IRL, 2213gt/77) was passing Battery Point in early 1995, her cargo including a neat line of the compar containers on deck. The ship was built in Japan by the Kagoshima Dock and Works Co Ltd, and was lengthened in 1984. Ironically, after the collapse of Lines, she returned to the Far East and now works under the name **Hai Xia Tong**.

e arrival on the Irish Sea of the **Bell Pioneer** (IRL, 6111gt/90) brought a new d innovative profile to the area. Not readily apparent when viewed from the ore is the fact that three of her four holds had no hatch covers; indeed she was claimed to be the world's first hatchless container ship. She has a container oacity of 303 TEU. Following the collapse of Bell Lines, she soon found new ners and currently trades in the Mediterranean linking ports in Italy and Greece to the Lebanon. Trade in these warm climes seemed unlikely when she was photographed on a bitterly cold January day in 1997 with frost lingering on the grassy embankment. At this time, she was trading between Avonmouth, Dublin and Radicatel on the River Seine. She was to be taken out of service and laid up in Newport only a few weeks later.

One very popular Bell Lines route was that which linked Avonmouth to Waterford. Seawheel took over this route and the **Christine O** (ATG, 1925gt/78) soon became a regular sight as she passed Battery Point linking the two ports and making two or three voyages each week. This continued until 2 October 2004 when the Seawheel service to Waterford ceased and her charter ended, being replaced by larger vessels which served Dublin rather than Waterford. However, the base cargo of this service, fibreboard, is still being imported from Waterford to Avonmouth but using conventional coasters. The ship was built at the pr[o] yard of J J Sietas on the outskirts of Hamburg. Originally named **John Bluh[r]** was under this name that she began the service between Avonmouth Waterford; she was renamed **Christine O** in mid-November 1998. In background is the **Yeoman Bank** whose details are on page 25. The photogr[a] was taken on 22 June 2004.

(D

s sometimes necessary to have good fortune when seeking photographs of ship passing another and the two photographs on this and the previous page examples of this fortune. On 24 April 2004, the **A. B. Amsterdam** (ATG, 44gt/97) was arriving from Garston to load 3665 tonnes of scrap in Avonmouth Bilbao. She was built at the Damen shipyard in Foxhol. Outward bound from

Royal Portbury Dock was the **Orion Leader** (PAN, 57513gt/99), built by Imabari Zosen K K, Marugame, which was heading for Zeebrugge having arrived with Mitsubishi cars from the Far East via Algiers the previous day. The new hull colours of NYK ships should be noted.

The pale yellow hulls of coastal vessels operated by F T Everard used to be a common sight in many ports throughout northern Europe. In recent years the company's fleet has consisted only of grey-hulled tankers, some of which do visit Avonmouth. A reminder of the days when the company owned dry cargo ships is provided by this photograph of the **Speciality** (BHS, 2822gt/77) hurrying up the channel with Swedish softwood on 19 August 1999. Built at Goole, she is also reminder of the time when the UK had a proud shipbuilding tradition. In 2002, she was sold out of the Everard fleet as the company began to concentrate on trades. She was renamed **Elen** and in early 2004 became **Goodway** and usually trades in the Mediterranean.

The Liverpool-registered **Briarthorn** (GBR, 1576gt/80) was built at the Richards yard in Lowestoft. She carries the funnel colours of S William Coe as she heads up channel in ballast from Belfast on 3 November 1993, departing for the same port two days later after loading her cargo of grain. This company had merged its fleet with that of Metcalf Motor Coasters and by the end of the decade had become part of the Barrow-based James Fisher group. During the first three years of the new millennium, several long-established UK shipowners disposed of their dry cargo vessels as already noted on the previous page. The **Briarthorn** was sold for trade in the Mediterranean in 2002 and was renamed **O. K. Apostolos**. At the time of the photograph, there was little evidence of any construction work on the new Severn Bridge.

The crystal clear winter air on 19 December 1999 ensured fine views of the snow-covered hills in South Wales as the *Harns* (NLD, 1909gt/94) passed the Point on her way up channel. The three chimneys of Uskmouth power station are prominent in the distance. These have been reduced to just a single chimney following the demolition of a section of this power station. Interestingly, the *Harns* is carrying heavy generating units built by Siemens in Germany and shipped from Duisburg to Avonmouth. She was one of a series of RMS vessels which calle the late 1990s with transformers, turbines and generators for power station Didcot and Seabank. The ship was built at the Peters shipyard in Kampen an on charter to RMS, the letters standing for Rhein, Maas SeeSchiffahrtskantor, based in Duisburg and one of the largest compan involved in chartering small coasters and inland waterway vessels.

s photograph was taken on 7 April 2002 from a similar vantage point to the vious photograph, but some three years later. The **Georgette Trader** (ATG, 1gt/84) is an example of a standard class of coaster built in considerable nbers at the Hugo Peters shipyard in Wewelsfleth on the River Stör, a tributary of the mighty River Elbe. She was carrying 1290 tonnes of medium density fibreboard for discharge at Berth 2 in Royal Portbury Dock. Careful observation will show that the number of chimneys at Uskmouth power station has been reduced to just one and that other buildings have also been demolished.

The ***Sea Endeavour*** was an astonishing survivor, her name a reminder of the local towage company C J King & Sons Ltd whose colours she wears here. She was built by Richards (Shipbuilders) Ltd in 1980 and her arrival in the King fleet made a total of six tugs. In February 1983, the King fleet merged with that of Cory Ship Towage Ltd to form Cory-King Towage and she was one of only two King tugs to join the new fleet, still bearing KIng colours when this photograph was taken in June 1984. She later wore two variants of the Cory livery. In 2000, Cory Towage was taken over by the Dutch Wijsmuller company and the ***Endeavour*** adopted this company's vivid blue colours (see pages 65 and (Within 18 months, Wijsmuller was taken over by Svitzer, a Danish tow company and subsidiary of the huge Mærsk group. She was then repainte(Svitzer colours! In mid-2003, she was rendered redundant following the arriva two new tugs and retired to Swansea.

Point Gilbert was constructed at the Richard Dunston yard in Hessle, near ... She was one of a group of tugs built in the early 1970s to serve the Come- Chance oil refinery in Canada. Having worked there for almost seven years, **Point Gilbert** returned to the UK and joined the Avonmouth fleet, along with ...er vessel **Point James**, in June 1980. In 1986, the propulsion and towing equipment of the **Point Gilbert** were modified to allow her to work more effectively as a stern tug for the larger vessels then using Royal Portbury Dock. This photograph was taken in October 1993. By 2002, she had been replaced by more modern tugs and she transferred to the Cory fleet on the River Clyde.

The **Portgarth** is an example of a standard tug built by the prolific Damen company in The Netherlands. She represents a type designated ASD 3110, and is the first tug delivered to British owners by the Damen group. Launched at the company's yard in Gorinchem on 23 February 1995, she arrived in the Br[i]... Channel in the spring of that year. The photograph was taken on 6 Septem[ber] 1997.

ing up position on the starboard side of the bulk carrier *Zella Oldendorff* on May 2001 is the *Shannon* in full Wijsmuller colours. She was built by McTay ine at Bromborough as *Eldergarth* and was initially stationed on the Mersey. r transfer to an associate Irish company for work at Foynes and other ports on the Shannon estuary, she was appropriately renamed *Shannon*. On returning to the UK, she was sent to the Avonmouth fleet and retained the name *Shannon* despite rumours that she would revert to *Eldergarth*. She left the area to work on the Clyde in 2002.

The tugs did not remain in the Wijsmuller livery for very long for the Dutch company itself was taken over by Svitzer, a Danish tug operator, and the tugs soon began to be painted in this company's livery although the change was gradual. A glance at the funnel of the **Stackgarth** shows that by the date of this photograph, 24 March 2002, a Maltese cross had been painted on. This is a feature of the Svitzer funnel markings. The **Stackgarth** has an interesting history. Built in 1985 at the Richards shipyard in Great Yarmouth, she is one of a group of tugs built for use on the River Tees and considered to be of revolutio design when introduced. In 1994, she was transferred to Milford Haven, and the late 1990s saw her in service on the Mersey, Belfast and Swansea be moving to the Avonmouth fleet in summer 1999. She underwent so modifications to machinery and upperworks to make her more suited for wor this area.

ween April and November 2003, the Italian tug **Uran**, built in 1998 by Astilleros
on at Navia, was chartered from owners in Trieste pending the arrival of the
newly-built tugs **Svitzer Bristol** and **Svitzer Brunel**. She remained in her

owner's colours during her stay but she was renamed **Danegarth**. She and the
Westgarth are taking care of the stern of the bulk carrier **Yong Tong** on 3 August
2003.

The arrival of the **Avongarth** in the local tug fleet in the mid-1990s represented a new era for she is an example of a design very popular in Japan. She was built at Kobe in 1980 and when purchased by Cory Towage she was delivered to the UK as deck cargo on a heavy-lift ship. Before entering service locally, she was refitted at Sharpness. She and the **Westgarth** had a local reputation as being two noisiest tugs in the fleet until fitted with silencers! The photograph was ta on 17 January 2004.

(D

Svitzer Bristol and sister tug *Svitzer Brunel* represent the latest stage of design in the local fleet. They were built in Spain by Astilleros Zamakona, of ̤aya, and they arrived in the Bristol Channel respectively during July 2003 September 2003. Cory Towage and its predecessors had always used traditional names connected with the local area but Svitzer introduced a new naming scheme with these two tugs. The photograph is dated 30 November 2003, and the *Lass Mars* can just be seen in the distance on her way up to Sharpness.

The **Welsh Piper** (GBR, 1251gt/87), built at Appledore, has the distinction of being the first self-discharging dredger to be constructed for use in the Bristol Channel. The title of her owning company has changed over the years as takeovers have affected the sand trade. She is currently operated by British Dredging Ltd which is part of the RMC Aggregates group. The sand trade is now firmly based within the Avonmouth Old Dock following transfer from ... Bristol's city centre in the 1990s. She was photographed as she sailed ... dredging grounds on 14 January 2004.

City of Cardiff (GBR, 2074gt/97) can be found visiting many ports along the south and west coasts of England and Wales from Portsmouth to Heysham. She and sistership *City of Chichester* were built by Appledore Shipbuilders. Here we see her on her way to Avonmouth in April 2000. UMA is a partner with Hanson Aggregates in Bristol Channel Aggregates on a site alongside the disused lock entrance into Avonmouth Old Dock.

other company to dredge sand and aggregates from the Bristol Channel has en United Marine Aggregates (UMA) although this company has traditionally ved the Welsh side of the Bristol Channel rather than the English side. wever, as the size of dredgers increased during the 1980s and 1990s and the nber of smaller vessels declined, the new larger vessels traded further afield the local sand companies agreed a pooling arrangement for the imports. The

The **Arco Dart** (GBR, 1309gt/90) is another self-discharging sand dredger. Built at Sliedrecht in The Netherlands by IHC Holland, along with sistership **Arco Dee**, her original owners were ARC Marine, itself an offspring of the Amey Roadstone Company. ARC was subsumed into the empire of Hanson Aggregates and it is this company's colours that the dredgers now carry. However when this photograph was taken on 20 August 1995, she was still in the colours of ARC

Marine. With a capacity of some 1300 tonnes of sand, the dredgers w[e]re designed to be able to discharge quickly, allowing them to arrive, discharge a[nd] sail on the same tide in many ports. Although most of the sand is brought [to] Avonmouth, the **Arco Dart** and **Arco Dee** sometimes load at a sandbank off [the] port entrance and take this fine grade of sand to ports in South Wales.

An unusual arrival on 2 October 1999 was the research vessel **Challenger** (GBR, 5gt/73) which was noted as she made her way towards Avonmouth at the end a voyage from Southampton. Built at the James Lamont shipyard in Port sgow, the vessel was operated by the Natural Environment Research Council was equipped to undertake both fishery and hydrographic research. She arrived at Avonmouth to lay up and await sale, eventually departing for Liverpool on 2 July 2000. She was sold to other UK owners, and was renamed **SV Explorer**. Initially rumours suggested that her owners were intending to use her in research work on the **Titanic**.

Built at the Adriatico shipyard in Trieste as a passenger vessel, the ***Anastasis*** (MLT, 11701gt/53) was named ***Victoria*** until 1978. She is now the world's largest non-governmental hospital ship and is operated by Maritime Mercy Ministries Ltd and her main work is field assignments in poorer countries of the world where her medical facilities are put to good use. These facilities include three operating theatres, a dental clinic and a 44-bed hospital ward. The ship also provides base support for onshore projects involving community development teams. In addi to this field work which takes up about two-thirds of the ship's time, she a undertakes public relations tours and summer 1994 was spent in Europe. only is she visited by the general public who are made aware of her work but also receives donations of supplies. She was photographed as she pas Battery Point on 30 August 2002.

New Generation (GBR, 2355gt/66) was one of a pair of vessels built at the [...]l, Russell shipyard in Aberdeen for charter to what was then the Central [...]ctricity Generating Board. Named **Kingsnorth Fisher** until 1990, she and her [...]tership **Aberthaw Fisher** were designed to carry heavy loads such as transformers and generators used in power stations. These units remained on a heavy trailer and were towed off by specialist tractor units. On her final visit to the port, she carried the internal aircraft lift of an aircraft carrier. Sold and renamed **New Gen** in June 2001, she was scrapped not long afterwards.

The decommissioning of the Royal Yacht **Britannia** in the mid-1990s was controversial but it was felt that the expense of maintaining the ship outlived her usefulness even though she could be used as a hospital ship in time of war. To complete her career, she made a visit to many ports around the UK and she is seen arriving at Portbury on 2 June 1995. She visited Bristol several tim including the opening ceremony of the new "West Dock" on 8 August 1977. T Queen named the dock Royal Portbury Dock in the presence of local dignitar and port workers. The vessel is now preserved and open to visitors at Leith.

of the most familiar sights in the Bristol Channel during the early and late [sum]mer is the paddle steamer **Waverley** (693gt/47) which is replaced during the summer season by her running mate **Balmoral**. The vessels offer excellent [opp]ortunities to sail on the Bristol Channel and are descendants of the much-[love]d Campbell steamers, remembered by thousands of day trippers from a [prev]ious generation. The **Waverley** was built by A & J Inglis Ltd, Glasgow, for service on the River Clyde. She was sold in the mid-1970s for the princely sum of £1 to the Paddle Steamer Preservation Society. Since then, the PSPS has supported the ship's operating company and has helped to raise huge sums of money to keep the ship in working order and meet all current stringent safety requirements. She was photographed on on 2 June 1995 when she accompanied the Royal Yacht **Britannia**.

With busy main channels used by some very large vessels as they navigate through the sandbanks of the Bristol Channel, it is essential that the buoys are serviced on a regular basis. This work is undertaken by Trinity House and its buoy tender *Mermaid* (GBR, 2820gt/87) is seen approaching the Newcombe Buoy marking the northern limit of the navigable channel off Battery Point. The was built by Hyundai Heavy Industries at Ulsan in Korea. During 2004, T House announced that it was making passenger accommodation available one of its ships, the *Patricia*.

many years, the **Glen Avon** (GBR, 859gt/69) was a familiar sight passing ry Point on her way from her dedicated berth on the bank of the River Avon upstream of the Avon Bridge to discharge effluent in the lower Bristol nel. In the late 1990s, EU legislation forbade this practice and all such rs were taken out of service. By this time, though, the South West Water

Authority had already disposed of the **Glen Avon** for she was sold in 1994 to owners in Lagos by whom she was renamed **Olokun 2**. Built at the Troon yard of Ailsa Shipbuilders, she sported several hull colours during her later years in service but perhaps this bright blue hull suited her best.

Appropriately for our final view we see Battery Point in the late evening but it is from the water rather than from the Point itself. The vehicle carrier **St Barbara** (MLT, 27087gt/80) heads towards Royal Portbury Dock on 7 June 2004 at the end of a voyage from Antwerp. The ship was built by the Kurushima Dockyard Co Ltd at Onishi in Japan. She has accommodation for 3000 cars. She has be regular visitor since January 2001 bringing Fiat and Alfa Romeo cars from Ita northern European ports.

(I